Leckie
the education publisher
for Scotland

Primary **Maths**
for **Scotland**

2nd Level Maths

2C

Practice Workbook 1

© 2024 Leckie

001/01082024

10 9 8 7 6 5 4 3 2 1

ISBN 9780008680374

Published by
Leckie
An imprint of HarperCollins Publishers
Westerhill Road, Bishopbriggs, Glasgow, G64 2QT

T: 0844 576 8126 F: 0844 576 8131
leckiescotland@harpercollins.co.uk www.leckiescotland.co.uk

HarperCollins Publishers
Macken House, 39/40 Mayor Street Upper, Dublin 1, D01 C9W8, Ireland

Publisher: Fiona McGlade

Special thanks
Project editor: Peter Dennis
Layout: Jouve
Proofreader: Julianna Dunn

A CIP Catalogue record for this book is available from the British Library.

Acknowledgements
Images © Shutterstock.com

Printed in India by Multivista Global Pvt. Ltd.

Contents

Answers
Check your answers to this workbook online: https://collins.co.uk/pages/scottish-primary-maths

1.1 Rounding whole numbers

1 In the boxes, write the two multiples of 10000 that come before and after each number.

Draw an ↓ showing where you think the actual number lies on the number line and round each number to the nearest 10000.

a) 37 252 lies between [30 000] and [40 000] rounds to [ ]

b) 637 252 lies between [ ] and [ ] rounds to [ ]

c) 657 252 lies between [ ] and [ ] rounds to [ ]

d) 35 049 lies between [ ] and [ ] rounds to [ ]

2 Round these numbers to the nearest 100 000. Draw an empty number line to help if required.

a) 426 209 rounded [ ]

b) 456 209 rounded [ ]

c) 556 209 rounded [ ]

d) 624 195 rounded [ ]

e) 724 195 rounded [ ]

f) 784 500 rounded [ ]

3 Finlay and Nuria have been rounding numbers. They notice that they have written different answers for some of the questions. Look at the children's answers and decide which are correct and which are incorrect.

	Number to round	Finlay	Nuria
a)	284 967	280 000	300 000
b)	52 914	50 000	50 000
c)	773 820	770 000	770 000
d)	350 906	300 000	300 000

Write the correct answers into the boxes below and tick the name of the child you agree with.

Finlay   Nuria

a) 284 967 rounded to the nearest 100 000 ⬚ ☐ ☐

b) 52 914 rounded to the nearest 10 000 ⬚ ☐ ☐

c) 773 820 rounded to the nearest 10 000 ⬚ ☐ ☐

d) 350 906 rounded to the nearest 100 000 ⬚ ☐ ☐

★ **Challenge**

1. Use these clues to find the correct number from the eight possibilities. Circle your answer.

446 371	386 421	320 465	366 251
403 862	488 231	43 284	411 840

- I am a six-digit number.
- I have exactly 4 even digits, but I am odd.
- When you round me to the nearest 10 000, I round up.
- I am 400 000 when rounded to the nearest 100 000.

2. Use these clues to find the correct number from the eight possibilities. Circle your answer.

852 185	78 145	819 445	749 315
793 604	776 825	802 218	830 560

- When you round me to the nearest 10 000, I round down.
- I am a multiple of 5.
- I am 800 000 when rounded to the nearest 100 000.

1.2 Rounding decimal fractions

1 Round each of these decimal numbers to the nearest hundredth:

a) 4·732 rounds to [ ]

b) 4·734 rounds to [ ]

c) 4·737 rounds to [ ]

d) 4·735 rounds to [ ]

e) 4·7316 rounds to [ ]

f) 74·738 rounds to [ ]

2 Circle True or False for each number statement.
Write the correct answer in the answer box for those that are false.

a) 5·623 rounded to the nearest hundredth is 5·63   **True   False**   [ ]

b) 5·693 rounded to the nearest hundredth is 5·69   **True   False**   [ ]

c) 5·616 rounded to the nearest hundredth is 5·62   **True   False**   [ ]

d) 25·185 rounded to the nearest hundredth is 25·19   **True   False**   [ ]

e) 25·183 rounded to the nearest hundredth is 25·180   **True   False**   [ ]

3 Round these measurements to two decimal places:

a) 2·059 litres [ ]

b) 81·488 kg [ ]

c) 0·073 cm [ ]

d) 418·571 km [ ]

1. Circle the numbers that give 37·43 when rounded to the nearest hundredth. One has been done for you.

37·421   37·435   37·4218   37·4302   37·429   37·4306

2. Find as many six-digit decimal numbers as you can that give 8·29 when rounded to the nearest hundredth.

1.3 Using rounding to estimate the answer

1 Amman has worked out these problems. Use rounding and estimating to help you to decide if his answers are reasonable. Explain your thinking for each one. The first one has been done for you.

a) $17\,428 - 4283 = 13\,145$

⟨Reasonable⟩	Not Reasonable	Rounding to the nearest 1000, this is $17\,000 - 4000$. $13\,000$ is a good estimate so $13\,145$ is reasonable.

b) $36 \times 18 = 928$

Reasonable	Not Reasonable	

c) $24\,740 + 5429 = 30\,169$

Reasonable	Not Reasonable	

d) $72\,375 - 23\,862 = 48\,513$

Reasonable	Not Reasonable	

e) $45 \times 21 = 9540$

Reasonable	Not Reasonable	

f) $275\,812 - 122\,401 = 153\,411$

Reasonable	Not Reasonable	

2 Say whether each answer is reasonable or not. Explain your answer.

	Reasonable		Explain your answer
	Yes	No	
Zahid multiplied 48 by 9 and got 432.			
Alana multiplied 79 by 6 and got 513.			
Marek multiplied 93 by 7 and got 651.			

★ **Challenge**

Use estimation to help you here. Choose three numbers from those shown so that when you add them together the answer is close to 100 000. Do you think there is a better solution? Try a different set of three numbers.

68 416   71 829
    25 980
9817   81 904
    38 055
17 356   4203

2.1 Reading and writing whole numbers

1 Write these six-digit numbers in words.

a) 143 284

b) 143 519

c) 143 020

d) 743 020

e) 753 020

f) 700 020

2 Write these six-digit numbers in numerals.

a) eight hundred and twenty-five thousand, three hundred and seventy-one

b) eight hundred and five thousand, three hundred and seventy-one

c) two hundred and five thousand, three hundred and seventy-one

d) five hundred and five thousand, three hundred and seventy-one

e) five hundred thousand and thirteen

f) seven hundred and twenty-two thousand, nine hundred

3 This is the key for a secret code:

0	1	2	3	4	5	6	7	8	9
@	$	%	&	*	§	±	{	~	^

Work out the six-digit number. Write it in numerals and then in words.

a) | & | § | ± | { | @ | ^ |

b) | % | ~ | $ | ± | * | % |

c) | § | @ | & | ~ | & | @ |

6430102

In words, this number says **six million, four hundred and thirty thousand, one hundred and two**.

Write the number that is two million more than this number in both words and numerals.

2.2 Representing and describing whole numbers

1 Isla made the number 214 336 with place value arrow cards.

| 2 0 0 0 0 0 ▷ | 1 0 0 0 0 ▷ | 4 0 0 0 ▷ | 3 0 0 ▷ | 3 0 ▷ | 6 ▷ |

| 2 1 4 3 3 6 ▷ |

Nuria used place value counters to make the same number.

Write each number here in numerals. You can use place value arrow cards **or** place value counters to help you if necessary.

a) three hundred and twenty thousand, two hundred and fourteen

b) three hundred thousand, two hundred and fourteen

c) five hundred thousand, two hundred and fourteen

d) five hundred thousand, two hundred and four

2 For each number, write the value of the underlined digit in both words and numerals. The first one has been done for you.

a) 5<u>6</u>2 804   **Sixty thousand, 60 000**

b) <u>5</u>62 804

c) 562 80<u>4</u>

d) <u>3</u>18 241

e) 318 241

f) 318<u>2</u>41

g) 3<u>1</u>8 241

h) 9<u>6</u>0 377

3

| 4 | 7 | 0 | 1 | 8 | 5 |

Use the digits on these cards to find a number to match each clue.
Write your answer in words and numerals:

a) Find an even six-digit number with zero in the thousands place.
   Now write it in words.

b) Find the smallest six-digit number where the value of the 5 is 50.
   Now write it in words.

★ **Challenge**

Find the smallest number you can make
using **all** these cards.
Write your number in both words and numerals.

| four | and | fifty |

| thousand | hundred | million |

| eighteen | three |

1 The number 631 825 has been partitioned in six different ways (and more partitions are possible!)

$$600\,000 + 30\,000 + 1000 + 800 + 20 + 5$$

$$631\,000 + 800 + 20 + 5$$

$$630\,000 + 1000 + 800 + 20 + 5$$

631 825

$$631\,000 + 825$$

$$600\,000 + 31\,825$$

$$630\,000 + 1825$$

Find six different ways to partition each of these numbers.

641 825

541 825

541 625

2 Write the number represented by these place value houses in four different ways. The first one has been done for you.

a)

Thousands			Ones		
H	T	O	H	T	O
4	2	3	8	5	9

423 thousands, 8 hundreds, 5 tens and 9 ones.
423 thousands, 8 hundreds, 59 ones.
423 thousands, 85 tens and 9 ones.
423 thousands, 859 ones.

b)

Thousands			Ones		
H	T	O	H	T	O
4	2	3	2	5	9

c)

Thousands			Ones		
H	T	O	H	T	O
1	2	3	2	5	9

d)

Thousands			Ones		
H	T	O	H	T	O
1	2	3	2	4	9

★ Challenge

Nuria is partitioning the number 725 844. She says:

> I can partition this in two ways. It can be 725 thousands, 8 hundreds and 44 ones. It can also be 700 thousands, 258 hundreds and 4 ones.

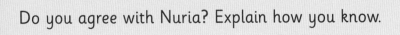

Do you agree with Nuria? Explain how you know.

2.4 Number sequences

1 Write the next five numbers in each sequence.

a) 528 286, 528 287, 528 288,

[ ] , [ ] , [ ] , [ ] , [ ]

b) 528 296, 528 297, 528 298,

[ ] , [ ] , [ ] , [ ] , [ ]

c) 528 996, 528 997, 528 998,

[ ] , [ ] , [ ] , [ ] , [ ]

d) 529 993, 529 994, 529 995,

[ ] , [ ] , [ ] , [ ] , [ ]

e) 549 997, 549 998, 549 999,

[ ] , [ ] , [ ] , [ ] , [ ]

f) 299 996, 299 997, 299 998,

[ ] , [ ] , [ ] , [ ] , [ ]

2 Now write the next five numbers in each of these sequences.

a) 712 314, 712 313, 712 312,

[ ] , [ ] , [ ] , [ ] , [ ]

b) 712 404, 712 403, 712 402,

[ ] , [ ] , [ ] , [ ] , [ ]

c) 712 006, 712 005, 712 004,

[ ] , [ ] , [ ] , [ ] , [ ]

d) 780006, 780005, 780004,

	,	,	,	,

e) 800006, 800005, 800004,

	,	,	,	,

f) 400002, 400001, 400000,

	,	,	,	,

3

Look at these number sequences. Are the numbers increasing or decreasing? How much bigger or smaller are they getting each time? One has been done for you.

Increasing means getting bigger. Decreasing means getting smaller.

a) 370004, 470004, 570004, 670004

The numbers are increasing. They get bigger by 100000 each time.

b) 413501, 413401, 413301, 413201

c) 175850, 174850, 173850, 172850

d) 599988, 599998, 600008, 600018

Amman and Isla made two number sequences. In their sequences they used the numbers on each of these cards only once. One sequence had four numbers in it and the other had five numbers in it. In one sequence the numbers were increasing and in the other sequence the numbers were decreasing. Write down what you think the two sequences were.

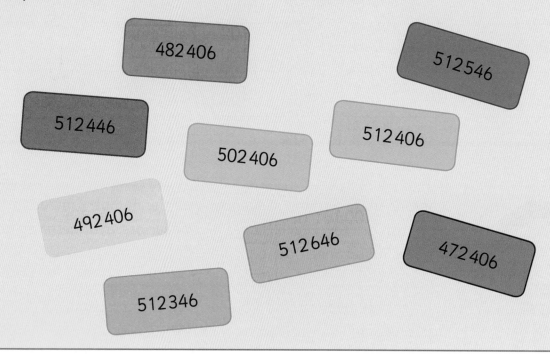

482 406

512 546

512 446

512 406

502 406

492 406

512 646

472 406

512 346

2.5 Comparing and ordering whole numbers

1 Write **<** or **>** in each box to make each statement true.

a) 420 381 [ ] 420 821

b) 200 720 [ ] 200 702

c) 634 100 [ ] 63 410

d) 508 650 [ ] 508 655

2 Circle True or False for each of these statements. Change some words in the false statements to make them true. Cross out the word you are changing and write the new word in the answer box.

a) 403 200 = four hundred and three thousand, two hundred   **True**   **False**

[ ]

b) 311 131 < three hundred thousand one hundred and eleven   **True**   **False**

[ ]

c) 602 544 > sixty-two thousand five hundred and forty-four   **True**   **False**

[ ]

d) 100 010 < ten thousand and ten   **True**   **False**

[ ]

3 Write each set of numbers in ascending order (smallest to largest).

a) 523 162   523 149   523 154   523 160   523 151

b) 187 960   187 951   187 966   187 909   187 941

c) 638 194   638 199   638 180   638 189   638 191

4

a) Use the numerals on the cards to make different six-digit numbers that fit the criteria.

0		5
4		9
3		6

- A multiple of 5

- An odd number

- The smallest possible number

- A multiple of 10

- An even number

- A multiple of 25

b) Now put your numbers in descending order (largest to smallest).

1. Use these cards to make nine different six-digit numbers.

Four hundred and seventeen thousand...	...three hundred and twenty-five
Two hundred and forty-one thousand...	...three hundred and fifty-two
Four hundred and forty-one thousand...	...two hundred and eighteen

2. Write all nine numbers in ascending order (smallest to largest).

2.6 Negative numbers

1 These tables show the midday temperature on 1st December in some European cities.

Athens	12°C
Brussels	2°C
Cologne	−1°C
Edinburgh	3°C

Helsinki	−5°C
Istanbul	7°C
Kyiv	−4°C
Lisbon	11°C

Oslo	−3°C
Paris	0°C
Rome	5°C
Zurich	−2°C

1. In which cities was the midday temperature below freezing?

2. Which city had the coldest midday temperature on this day?

3. How many degrees warmer was it in Rome than in Oslo?

4. Athens was 14°C warmer than which city?

5. What was the difference in temperature between Lisbon and Kyiv?

6. What was the difference in temperature between the coldest and the warmest places?

7. Write the names of the cities in order, from coldest to warmest.

A diver uses an underwater drone to take some photos of a shipwreck. The depth that each photo was taken at is shown here:

Draw a picture of the underwater scene and label it with these depths in the correct order.

2.7 Reading and writing decimal fractions

1 Match each of these decimal fractions with the correct speech bubble. One has been done for you.

6·105

0·615

26·615

200·003

230·103

13·315

> two hundred and thirty point one zero three

> twenty-six point six one five

> thirteen point three one five

> six point one zero five

> zero point six one five

> two hundred point zero zero three

2 4 wholes and 183 thousandths can be written as 4·183

	Ones				Decimal Fractions		
H	T	O	.	$\frac{1}{10}$	$\frac{1}{100}$	$\frac{1}{1000}$
		4	.	1	8	3

Write in numerals:

a) 7 wholes and 351 thousandths

b) 7 wholes and 391 thousandths

c) 27 wholes and 391 thousandths

d) 27 wholes and 396 thousandths

e) 52 wholes and 184 thousandths

f) 0 wholes and 485 thousandths

g) 257 wholes and 5 thousandths

h) 9 wholes and 46 thousandths

★ Challenge

A new activity area has a piece of play equipment that measures 4·950 metres high. Isla says "That is 4 metres and 950 thousandths of a metre". Amman says "No, it is 4 metres and 95 thousandths of a metre". Who do you think is correct? Explain. You can use the place value houses to help you.

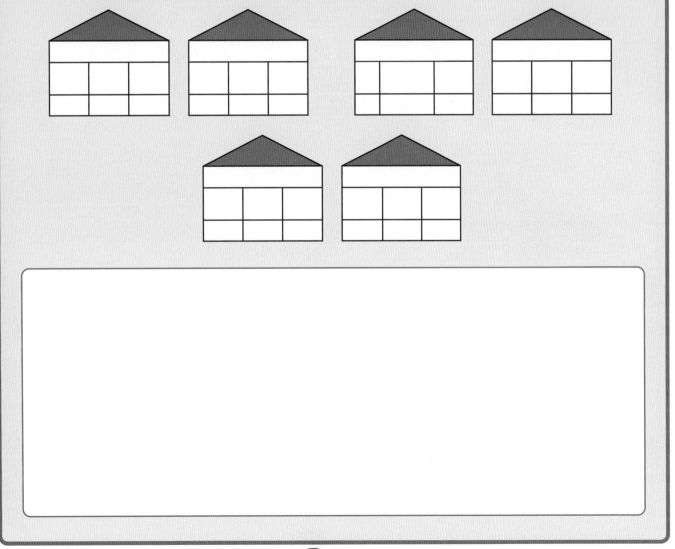

2.8 Representing and describing decimal fractions

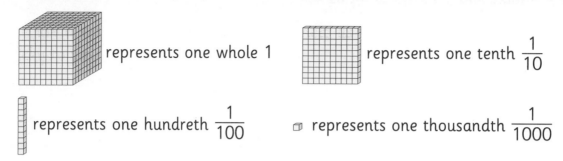

represents one whole 1

represents one tenth $\frac{1}{10}$

represents one hundreth $\frac{1}{100}$

represents one thousandth $\frac{1}{1000}$

This model represents the decimal fraction 2·416

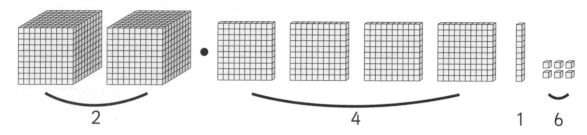

2   4   1   6

We can write this decimal fraction in three ways, like this:

2 ones, 4 tenths, 1 hundredth and 6 thousandths = 2·416 = $2\frac{416}{1000}$

---

1 Write the decimal fraction represented by the following models in three ways.

a)

b)

c)

d)

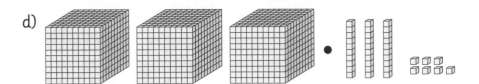

e)

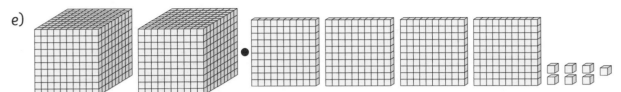

f)

★ Challenge

The children built a model of a decimal fraction with thousandths and then wrote
the decimal fraction in three different ways. They had to break the model down and
when they looked at their answers some paint had been spilled on the page. Can you
work out what the decimal fraction was?

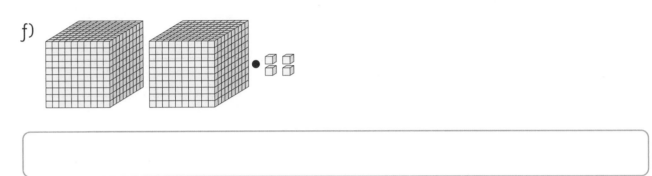

3 thousands = · 2 = $5\dfrac{}{1000}$

We will need

enths

9 hu

sands

2.9 Zero as a placeholder in decimal fractions

1 Describe the position of the placeholders in these decimal fractions.
For example:

23·004 → the placeholders are in the tenths and hundredths places

a) 30·185   The placeholders are

b) 30·085   The placeholders are

c) 30·005   The placeholders are

d) 296·107   The placeholders are

e) 206·007   The placeholders are

f) 801·530   The placeholders are

2 This diagram represents 1 whole and 37 hundredths.
We can write this as a fraction or as a decimal fraction.

$1\frac{37}{100}$ *one and thirty-seven hundredths*

1·37 *one point three seven*

Circle True or False for each of these. Rewrite the false statements to make them true.

a) $7·39 = 7\frac{39}{100}$ **True**   **False**

b) $7·09 = 7\frac{9}{1000}$ **True**   **False**

c) $7·095 = 7\frac{95}{1000}$ **True**   **False**

d) $15 \cdot 8 = 15\frac{8}{10}$ **True**   **False**

e) $30 \cdot 06 = 30\frac{6}{100}$ **True**   **False**

f) $41 \cdot 106 = 41\frac{16}{100}$ **True**   **False**

3. Using some or maybe all of the grids provided, draw a diagram to show each of these.

a) $0 \cdot 3 = 0 \cdot 30$

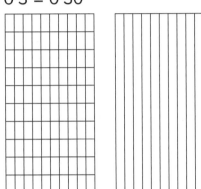

b) $0 \cdot 3 + 0 \cdot 04 = 0 \cdot 34$

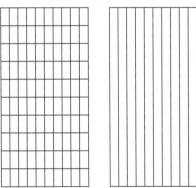

★ **Challenge**

1. Find as many pairs of equal numbers as you can. One has been done for you.

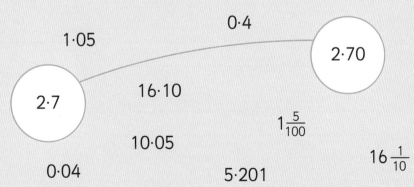

10·050

0·4

1·05

2·70

16·10

2·7

10·05

$1\frac{5}{100}$

0·04

5·201

$16\frac{1}{10}$

2. For the numbers without a pair, write a matching number on the diagram and join them up.

2.10 Partitioning decimal fractions

1 Write the decimal fraction that can be made using these place value arrow cards.

a) 3. 0·6 0·0 1 0·0 0 9

b) 5. 0·6 0·0 1 0·0 0 9

c) 5. 0·2 0·0 1 0·0 0 9

d) 5. 0·2 0·0 1 0·0 0 4

e) 0. 0·8 0·0 7 0·0 0 3

g) 0·0 0·0 4 0·0 0 2

2 Partition these decimal fractions. For example: **4·65 = 4 + 0·6 + 0·05**

a) 9·2

b) 9·7

c) 9·1

d) 7·61

e) 7·68

f) 7·08

g) 2·164

h) 2·144

i) 2·044

j) 6·005

★ Challenge

1. Match the place value counters to the correct decimal fraction.

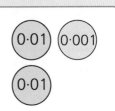

0·01 0·001

0·01

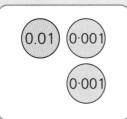

0·1 0·001

0·001

0·01 0·001

0·001

0·102   0·012   0·021

2. Now make up three examples of your own like this.

2.11 Comparing and ordering decimal fractions

1 Write these decimal fractions in order from smallest to largest.

a) 2·518   7·518   0·518   5·518   4·518

b) 6·273   6·573   6·073   6·773   6·173

c) 5·428   5·421   5·425   5·420   5·426

d) 0·754   0·479   0·27   0·081   0·603

2 Circle True or False for each of these statements. Change the symbol in the false statements to make them true.

a) 2·73 > 2·6   **True**   **False**

b) 16·4 = 16·40   **True**   **False**

c) 5·07 = 5·7   **True**   **False**

d) 8·3 < 8·14   **True**   **False**

e) 9·02 > 9·11   **True**   **False**

f) 7 = 7·000   **True**   **False**

3 Complete each of the following statements. The first one has been done for you.

a) 6 hundredths and 3 thousandths = [63] thousandths = [0·063]

b) 4 hundredths and 9 thousandths = [ ] thousandths = [ ]

c) 5 tenths and 8 hundredths and 0 thousandths = 58 [ ] = [ ]

d) 300 thousands = [ ] hundredths = [ ] tenths = 0·3

★ **Challenge**

Five children take part in a long jump event at an athletics competition. The lengths of their jumps are as follows:

3·094 m   3·1 m   3·64 m   3·09 m   3·52 m

1. How far was the longest jump? [ ]

2. List the jumps in order, starting with the smallest.

[ ]

3. Isla takes part in the event after these five children have jumped. She makes the second longest jump. What is the longest she could have jumped and the shortest she could have jumped?

[ ]

3.1 Mental addition and subtraction

1 Calculate using a mental strategy of your choice.

a) 13 478 + 999

b) 17 478 + 999

c) 17 478 + 1999

d) 26 300 + 491

e) 26 300 + 891

f) 31 278 + 3005

g) 16 600 − 398

h) 16 600 − 598

i) 16 600 − 1998

j) 42 765 − 304

k) 21 648 − 1009

l) 50 831 − 7002

Which mental strategy did you use most when doing these calculations? Explain your thinking to a partner.

2 Use place value and number facts to calculate each of these.

a) 104502 + 70000 _____

b) 104502 + 20000 _____

c) 304502 + 20040 _____

d) 701430 + 130021 _____

e) 678302 – 30000 _____

f) 678302 – 50000 _____

g) 293804 – 120200 _____

h) 580273 – 320001 _____

★ Challenge

1. What number is ten thousand more than 499900? _____

2. In 2020, the population of Glasgow was 632350 and the population of Edinburgh was 506520.

   a) What was the total population of both cities in 2020? _____

   b) How many more people were living in Glasgow than in Edinburgh at that time? _____

3.2 Adding and subtracting a string of numbers

1 Add these strings of numbers.

a) 347 + 53 + 12 + 8000 + 2000 + 426

b) 347 + 53 + 12 + 9000 + 2000 + 426

c) 447 + 53 + 12 + 9000 + 2000 + 426

d) 2300 + 70 + 730 + 1700 + 391 + 29

e) 2300 + 60 + 740 + 1700 + 391 + 29

f) 2700 + 60 + 740 + 1300 + 391 + 29

g) 185 + 1445 + 68 + 632 + 2555 + 15

2 Find the missing digits in each of these calculations and fill them in to complete the number sentences.

a) 3273 + 1☐☐☐ + 607 = 4920

b) 7☐☐☐ − 420 − 380 = 6560

3 Subtract each set of numbers from the starting number in bold.

a) Start with **16 380**. Subtract 280, 316 and 154 from this number.

b) Start with **14 270**. Subtract 280, 316 and 154 from this number.

c) Start with **14 270**. Subtract 290, 326 and 144 from this number.

d) Start with **27 000**. Subtract 2038, 460 and 562 from this number.

e) Start with **35 050**. Subtract 2100, 85, 1900 and 115 from this number.

★ **Challenge**

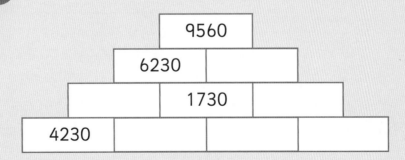

In this number pyramid, the number in each block is the total of the two numbers in the blocks below it. Find all the missing numbers.

3.3 Using place value partitioning to add and subtract

1 We can use an empty number line and partitioning into thousands, hundreds, tens and ones to help us add and subtract six-digit numbers. For example:

37 560 + 240 315

Start with 240 315 and partition 37 560 into 30 000 + 7000 + 500 + 60

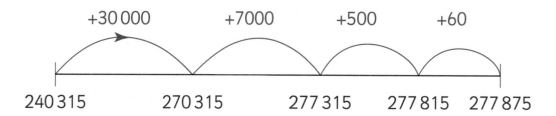

37 560 + 240 315 = 277 815

Use an empty number line and partitioning to calculate:

a) 108 463 + 47 315

b) 25 374 + 53 481

c) 108 463 + 43 315

d) 108 463 + 63 315

e) 59 230 + 380 610

g) 47 249 − 23 136

f) 83 564 − 32 173

h) 145 628 − 32 173

i) 145 628 − 91 329

j) 473 525 − 418 361

2 We can also use the column method to help us add and subtract six-digit numbers.
For example:

$$736\,423 - 424\,306$$

```
      736 423
  –   424 306
      300 000
       10 000
        2 000
          100
           20
  –        3
      312 117
```

Use this method to calculate:

a) 25 674 + 23 481

b) 162 481 + 241 537

c) 147 249 – 113 255

d) 635 816 – 521 809

Choose a suitable method to work out each of these.

a) 492 517 + 186 374

b) 863 795 − 704 518

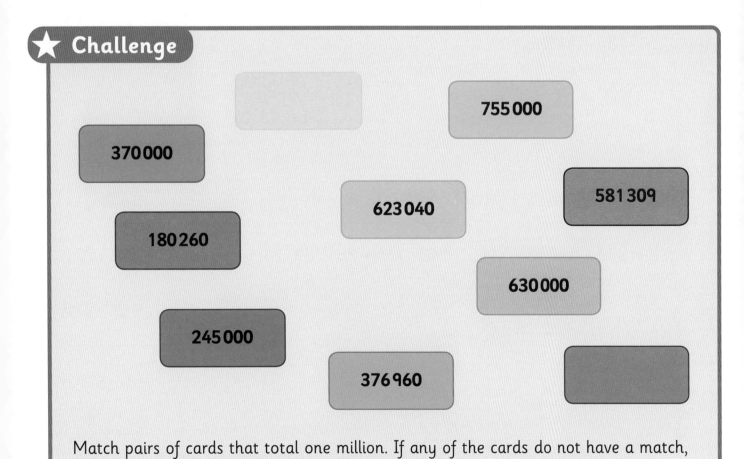

★ Challenge

755 000

370 000

581 309

623 040

180 260

630 000

245 000

376 960

Match pairs of cards that total one million. If any of the cards do not have a match, write the matching number on one of the blank cards.

3.4 Adding whole numbers using standard algorithms

1 We can use a standard written algorithm to help us with addition calculations that are too tricky to work out mentally. For example:

35 416 + 17 836 + 28 533

```
    2 1    1
   35 416
   17 836
 + 28 533
   81 785
```

Use a standard written algorithm to work out the answer to each of these additions.

a) 47 108 + 38 265

b) 47 168 + 38 295

c) 47 568 + 38 895

d) 637 184 + 44 296

e) 637 184 + 144 296

f) 284 377 + 510 384

g) 294 377 + 540 384

h) 437 113 + 351 782

i) 437 113 + 391 782

2 Calculate the answers to these questions using the standard written algorithm for addition.

a) 41 267 + 37 482 + 12 866

b) 41 767 + 37 582 + 12 466

c) 71 767 + 47 582 + 32 466

d) 8462 + 175 355 + 36 714

3 These written algorithms contain some errors. Identify the errors then rewrite each algorithm correctly.

a)
```
  1 1 1
  1 7 4 8 2
+     4 6 9 1
  _____
  1 1 0 7 3
```

b)
```
          1
    2 3  4 8 3
+   2 5  6 7 6
  _____
  4 8 1  1 5 9
```

c)
```
      1  1
  1 2  9 3
+ 3 0  4 7 1
  _____
  4 3  4 0 1
```

Fill in the missing digits in each of these written algorithms.

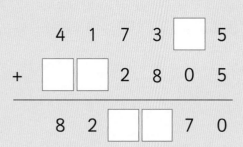

$$
\begin{array}{r}
8\ \boxed{3}\ 7\ 9\ 6 \\
+\ \boxed{9}\ 3\ \boxed{6}\ 2\ 9 \\
\hline
1\ 7\ 7\ 4\ \boxed{2}\ 5 \\
\hline
\end{array}
$$

$$
\begin{array}{r}
8\ 9\ 5\ 6\ 3 \\
+\ 4\ \boxed{3}\ 5\ \boxed{5}\ 9 \\
\hline
\boxed{1}\ \boxed{3}\ 3\ \boxed{1}\ 2\ 2 \\
\hline
\end{array}
$$

$$
\begin{array}{r}
4\ 1\ 7\ 3\ \boxed{6}\ 5 \\
+\ \boxed{4}\ \boxed{0}\ 2\ 8\ 0\ 5 \\
\hline
8\ 2\ \boxed{0}\ \boxed{1}\ 7\ 0 \\
\hline
\end{array}
$$

$$
\begin{array}{r}
\boxed{2}\ 6\ 6\ \boxed{3}\ 4\ 8 \\
5\ 4\ \boxed{6}\ 9\ 0\ 1 \\
+\ 6\ \boxed{3}\ 4\ 5\ 9\ 0 \\
\hline
\boxed{1}\ 4\ 7\ 7\ 8\ \boxed{3}\ 9 \\
\hline
\end{array}
$$

1 We can use a standard written algorithm to help us with subtraction calculations that are too tricky to work out mentally. For example:

48 217 − 29 632

```
    3 17 11 1
    4 8 2 1 7
  − 2 9 6 3 2
    1 8 5 8 5
```

Use a standard written algorithm to work out the answer to each of these subtractions.

a) 53 824 − 16 532

b) 53 824 − 16 537

c) 653 824 − 446 537

d) 623 824 − 446 537

e) 180 743 − 29 588

f) 473 120 − 38 202

g) 728 541 − 534 146

h) 803 400 − 256 315

2 Now, use a standard written algorithm to work out the answer to each of these subtractions. Check your answers by adding, like this:

48 217 − 29 632

```
    3 17 11  1
    4̷ 8̷ 2̷ 1 7          CHECK        1  1  1
  − 2 9 6 3 2   ← Add            2 9 6 3 2
  ─────────────                + 1 8 5 8 5
    1 8 5 8 5  ←                ─────────────
                                  4 8 2 1 7
```

a) 75 253 − 45 377

b) 75 053 − 45 877

c) 275 053 − 45 874

d) 215 053 − 145 874

e) 317 950 − 56 271

f) 317 950 − 156 271

These written algorithms contain some errors. Identify the errors then rewrite each algorithm correctly.

a)
```
   4 5 2 9 6
 – 1 8 4 0 8
 ─────────
   3 3 2 9 2
```

b)

```
    0  12 13  1
   1  3  4  1 7 3
 –  8  5  2 0 1
 ────────────
    4  6  9 7 2
```

c)

```
    0  15 15  1
   2  1  1  6 0 4
 – 1 0 8  8 4 1
 ────────────
   1 0 7  7 6 3
```

★ **Challenge**

1. Fill in the missing digits in each of these written algorithms.

```
    8   6   3   1   2
 –  ☐   7   ☐   7   ☐
   ─────────────────
    6   ☐   1   ☐   8
```

```
    ☐   ☐   4   ☐   9
 –  5   2   ☐   3   5
   ─────────────────
    1   8   8   9   4
```

2. Can you make up a missing digits subtraction of your own using five-digit numbers?

1 Calculate the following, choosing an efficient strategy for each one. Explain how you worked each answer out. Was it: partitioning, empty number line, mental calculation, algorithm, grouping or another strategy?

a) 130 000 + 270 000

b) 243 000 + 151 998

c) 430 000 + 10 001

d) 724 173 + 263 392

e) 398 745 + 400 020

f) 6284 + 3819 + 4537

2 Find the missing number on each brick in this subtraction pyramid by calculating the difference between the two numbers directly below it.

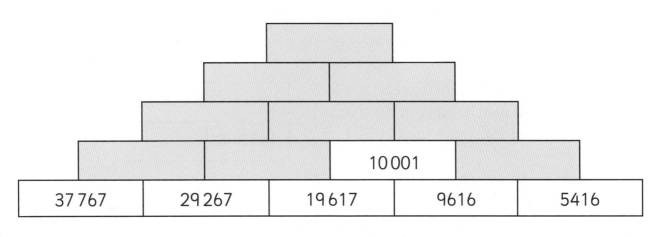

37 767	29 267	19 617	9616	5416

and inside the pyramid: 10 001

★ **Challenge**

1. Fill in the missing digits in each of these calculations.

    a) 3 ☐ 4 ☐ 1 + 1 800 = 34 20 ☐

    b) ☐ 7 ☐ 6 ☐ − 11 500 = 8 ☐ 963

2. Now create a missing digits subtraction calculation of your own using two five-digit numbers.

We can draw a Think Board to help us represent and solve a word problem, like this:

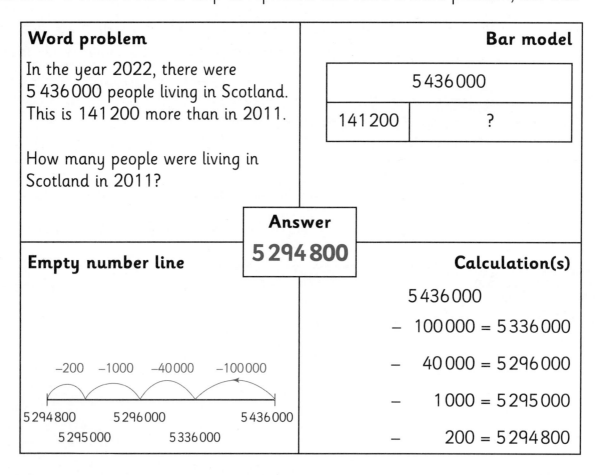

Complete the following Think Boards and solve each of these word problems.

1

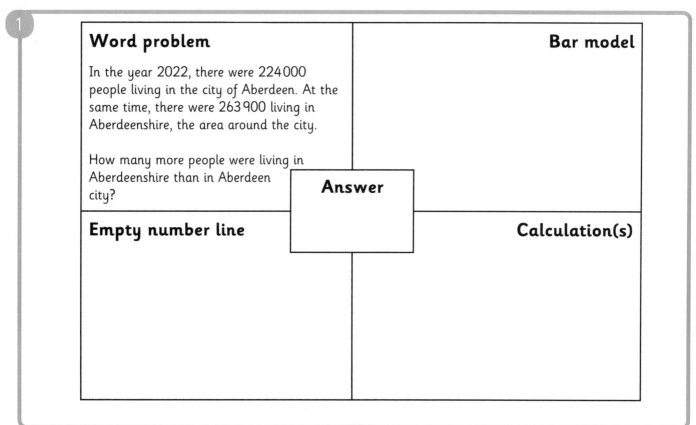

2

Word problem

In 2022, Cardiff was the largest city in Wales with a population of 485 340 and Swansea was the second largest city with a population of 381 300.
How many people altogether were living in Cardiff and Swansea at this time.

Bar model

Answer

Empty number line

Calculation(s)

3

Word problem

In January, February and March of 2022, 255 000 people visited Scotland. In the next three months of 2022, the number of visitors was 520 000.

How many people visited Scotland in April, May and June of 2022?

Bar model

Answer

Empty number line

Calculation(s)

4

Word problem	Bar model
In 2022, there were 832 300 people aged 15 and under living in Scotland. At the same time, 1 091 000 people over the age of 65 were living in Scotland. How many more over-65s were living in Scotland at that time?	
Empty number line	**Calculation(s)**

Answer

⭐ **Challenge**

Write a word problem for this partially completed Think Board.
Complete the Think Board for your word problem.

Word problem	Bar model
	342 600 28 400
Empty number line	**Calculation(s)**

Answer

3.8 Solving multi-step word problems

Solve each of these problems by breaking it down into steps.

1. A local animal rescue charity was given £164 300 to put towards building an animal shelter. A local business donated an additional £25 000 towards building the animal shelter. The cost of building the shelter is £208 500. How much more money will the animal rescue charity need to raise before the shelter can be built?

2. In one year, a children's theme park attracted 237 600 visitors. A nearby science centre had 34 870 visitors. Half of the science centre visitors said they had also gone to the theme park. How many visitors went to the theme park **only**?

3. 1000 visitors to a sea life centre were asked what their favourite creature was. $\frac{1}{4}$ chose otters, 430 chose sea lions, 185 chose turtles and the rest said sharks. How many of the 1000 visitors chose sharks as their favourite creature?

4 Amman, Findlay, Isla and Nuria are doing a step-count challenge as part of Health Week in school. The target for their team of four is to complete 400 000 steps in a week. They keep a note of their step count for the first six days of the challenge:

	Total after six days
Amman	88 407
Finlay	82 310
Isla	86 526
Nuria	87 521

a) How many steps does the team still have to complete to meet their target of 400 000?

b) On the final day of the challenge Findlay completes 12 453 steps and Nuria completes 14 467 steps. Amman and Isla decide that they will each do half of the remaining steps to get the team to 400 000. How many steps will Amman and Isla each need to complete?

This table shows the population of some European countries:

Country	Population
France	64 200 000
Germany	83 310 000
Italy	58 870 000
Spain	47 520 000
United Kingdom	67 500 000

Write the answer to each of these problems in numerals and words.

1. How many more people live in the United Kingdom than live in France?

2. How much lower is the population of Spain than of Italy?

3. What is the difference between the most populated and the least populated countries in the table?

3.9 Adding whole numbers and decimal fractions

1 We can **round** to the nearest ten to help us when we are adding whole numbers and decimal fractions. For example:

5·81 + 27 is the same as 2·81 + 30   **The answer is 32·81**

Use this strategy to calculate:

a) 49 + 7·53

b) 39 + 7·53

c) 39 + 4·53

d) 8·71 + 146

e) 8·93 + 146

f) 8·93 + 149

g) 27 + 14·62

h) 127 + 14·62

i) 258 + 18·78

j) 43·91 + 308

k) 56·33 + 419

l) 837 + 89·19

2 We can **round** to the nearest whole number and **compensate** to help us when we are adding decimal fractions. For example:

5·96 + 7·61 is the same as 6 + 7·57   The answer is 13·57

Use this strategy to calculate:

a) 6·97 + 2·56

b) 6·94 + 2·56

c) 8·94 + 2·56

d) 8·94 + 5·81

e) 8·94 + 5·91

f) 5·27 + 1·99

g) 5·27 + 3·97

h) 9·36 + 9·94

i) 3·99 + 7·99

j) 6·96 + 6·96

k) 0·85 + 0·99

3 We can **partition** each decimal fraction into whole numbers and hundredths to help us when we are adding decimal fractions. For example:

14·62 + 6·15 = 14 + 6 + 0·62 + 0·15 = 20 + 0·77 = 20·77

Use this strategy to calculate:

a) 15·23 + 8·41

b) 15·23 + 8·36

c) 17·23 + 8·36

d) 36·18 + 20·64

e) 36·44 + 20·17

f) 60·37 + 25·37

---

4 Calculate each of these using a mental strategy of your choice.

a) 3·97 + 6·82

b) 19 + 5·39

c) 45·17 + 27·31

d) 28·31 + 36

e) 9·41 + 7·98

[ ]

f) 19·38 + 29·51

[ ]

1. Find as many pairs of numbers as you can in this grid that add to make 2460·53. Join these up with a line on the grid. One has been done for you.

560·52	310·23	1060·42
2400	1400·11	1900·01
2150·30	1000·03	60·53

2. Are there any numbers that you have not used? If there are, work out what the matching number would be to make a pair that gives a total of 2460·53.

3.10 Adding decimal fractions using standard written algorithms

1 We can use a standard written algorithm to help us add decimal fractions that are too tricky to work out mentally. For example:

$245 \cdot 76 + 383 \cdot 59$

```
   1   1   1
   2 4 5 · 7 6
 + 3 8 3 · 5 9
   6 2 9 · 3 5
```

Use a standard written algorithm to find the answers to these additions.

a) 37·48 + 15·31

b) 37·88 + 15·31

c) 37·88 + 15·79

d) 163·74 + 48·68

e) 163·92 + 48·68

f) 17·08 + 318·93

g) 17·08 + 358·93

h) 62·17 + 118·66

i) 58·85 + 460·37

2 Calculate the answers to these questions using the standard algorithm for addition.

a) 7·53 + 28·49 + 1·67

b) 12·77 + 5·38 + 0·89

c) 23·61 + 18·78 + 38·97

d) 59·72 + 63·18 + 86·39

★ **Challenge**

Fill in the missing digits in each of these addition calculations.

1.
```
    ☐  4 · ☐  6
+   2  ☐ · 8  ☐
_____
    6  4 · 8  3
_____
```

2.
```
    ☐  2 · 9  ☐
    4  ☐ · 8  4
+   3  7 · ☐  9
_____
 1  4  0 · 3  9
_____
```

3.11 Subtracting decimal fractions

1 We can use place value partitioning to help us when we are subtracting decimal fractions. For example:

8·53 – 5·17

8 ones subtract 5 ones leaves **3 ones**

53 hundredths subtract 17 hundredths leaves **36 hundredths**

So, the answer is $3\frac{36}{100}$ = **3·36**

Use this method to calculate:

a) 5·74 – 3·16

b) 9·74 – 3·16

c) 28·56 – 8·43

d) 28·56 – 8·15

e) 52·93 – 12·08

f) 184·47 – 6·18

g) 285·82 – 9·73

2 We can use an empty number line and counting on when subtracting a decimal fraction from a whole number. For example:

13 – 5·18

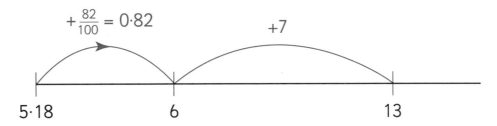

Count on from 5·18 to the next whole number, which is 6

5·18 + **0·82** = 6

Count on from 6 to 13, which is 7

6 + **7** = 13

So, 13 – 5·18 = 7·82

Use this method to calculate:

a) 12 – 4·82

b) 12 – 7·82

c) 12 – 7·39

d) 40 – 25·16

e) 43 − 25·16

f) 43 − 25·83

g) 43 − 35·83

h) 100 − 6·37

i) 500 − 45·81

j) 200 − 71·12

k) 700 − 94·54

l) 1000 − 38·62

3

a) Use the numbers on these starbursts to write six different subtractions.
For example, 2·73 – 1·06.

 1·06  **4**   **2·73**  **6·59**

b) Now calculate the answers to the subtractions you have made.
Explain the strategy you used for each one.

⭐ **Challenge**

Find three different pairs of numbers, each with a difference of 3·68.

65

3.12 Subtracting decimal fractions using standard algorithms

1 We can use a standard written algorithm to help us subtract decimal fractions that are too tricky to work out mentally. For example:

43·53 − 16·27

$$
\begin{array}{r}
^3\cancel{4}\,^1 3 \cdot \,^4\cancel{5}\,^1 3 \\
-\ 1\ 6 \cdot 2\ 7 \\
\hline
2\ 7 \cdot 2\ 6
\end{array}
$$

Use a standard written algorithm to calculate the following:

a) 36·53 − 17·61

b) 36·53 − 17·68

c) 36·19 − 17·68

d) 52·74 − 8·16

e) 52·04 − 8·16

f) 52·04 − 8·52

g) 73·82 − 6·92

h) 48·05 − 19·06

i) 29·17 − 23·86

j) 94·66 − 68·17

k) 50·05 − 33·82

l) 29·14 − 26·76

m) 38·04 − 28·77

n) 90·84 − 79·64

o) 63·91 − 39·96

---

2 Find the errors in this written algorithm and correct them.

$$
\begin{array}{r}
1\,7\cdot4\,6 \\
-\ 1\,1\cdot9\,1 \\
\hline
6\cdot5\,5 \\
\hline
\end{array}
$$

---

3 What is the missing number in this calculation?

17·27 − ☐ = 1·89

1. Fill in the missing digits in each of these subtraction calculations.

   a)
   $$
   \begin{array}{r}
   8\,\square\,.\,4\,\square \\
   -\ \square\,2\,.\,\square\,7 \\
   \hline
   4\ 7\,.\,4\ 9 \\
   \hline
   \end{array}
   $$

   b)
   $$
   \begin{array}{r}
   9\ 2\,.\,\square\,\square \\
   -\ \square\,\square\,.\,8\ 6 \\
   \hline
   3\ 4\,.\,5\ 7 \\
   \hline
   \end{array}
   $$

2. Now make up two mystery number questions and challenge a partner to solve them.

3.13 Adding and subtracting decimal fractions

1 Work out the answers to each of these additions using the most efficient method. For each one, say which method you used.

a) 14·73 + 3·2

b) 25·46 + 9·6

c) 6·4 + 34·03

d) 12·7 + 26·29

e) 67·4 + 35·83

f) 31·98 + 4·8

g) 136·2 + 5·67

h) 400·06 + 0·51

i) 207·42 + 30·79

j) 6·83 + 5·7 + 3·41

k) 4·5 + 8·8 + 10·4 + 17·52

2 Work out the answers to each of these subtractions using the most efficient method. For each one, say which method you used.

a) 6·1 – 3·85

b) 7·6 – 6·82

c) 4·1 – 0·02

d) 34·48 – 23·2

e) 16·4 – 2·98

f) 70·7 – 32·01

g) 45·76 – 30·4

h) 41·5 – 19·83

i) 26·08 – 4·3

j) 300 – 60·7

k) 150·9 – 14·61

l) 604·26 – 48·4

3 Write in the arrow what you must add or subtract from each input number to reach the output number. The first one has been done for you.

	INPUT		OUTPUT		INPUT		OUTPUT

a) 65·34 (+1) 66·34   b) 53·76 53·56

c) 18·71 18·77   d) 44·03 44·2

e) 83·89 83·69   f) 27·31  28·61

g) 51·8 50·62   h) 19·78 23·89

i) 39·69 33·62   j) 163·01 161·51

★ **Challenge**

Using each of the digits 1, 2, 3, 4, 5, 6, 7, 8 and 9 only once, complete this calculation.

$$0 \cdot \square\square\square$$
$$0 \cdot \square\square\square$$
$$+ \; 0 \cdot \square\square\square$$
$$\overline{}$$
$$0 \cdot 9 \; 9 \; 9$$

Complete a Think Board like this to represent and solve each of these word problems.

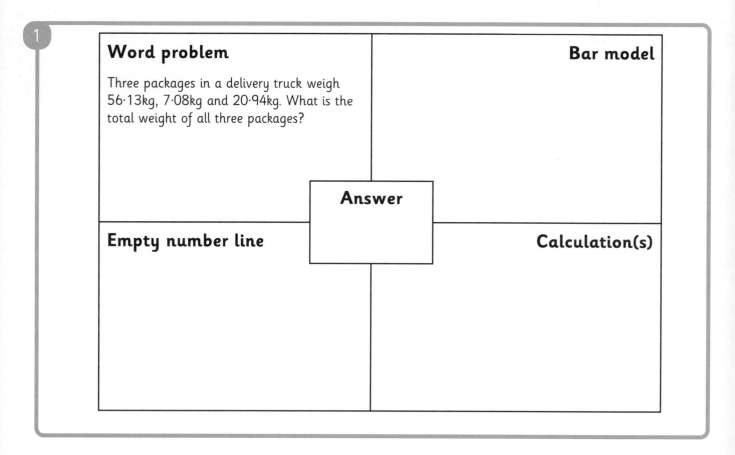

1

Word problem

Three packages in a delivery truck weigh 56·13kg, 7·08kg and 20·94kg. What is the total weight of all three packages?

Bar model

Answer

Empty number line

Calculation(s)

2

Word problem

Isla and Nuria are measuring how far they can throw a bean bag. Isla's throw measures 3·63m and Nuria's throw measures 4·17m.

How much further did Nuria throw the bean bag?

Bar model

Answer

Empty number line

Calculation(s)

3

Word problem

In an athletics competition the winner in the high jump set a new record by jumping 0·06m higher than the old record of 1·58m. What is the new high jump record?

Bar model

Answer

Empty number line

Calculation(s)

4

Word problem

The children grew three sunflowers in the school greenhouse. When they measured them they noted that the total height of the three sunflowers was 5·81m. Two of the sunflowers measured 2·07m and 1·92m. What was the height of the third sunflower?

Bar model

Answer

Empty number line

Calculation(s)

Write a word problem for this partially completed Think Board. Complete the Think Board for your word problem.

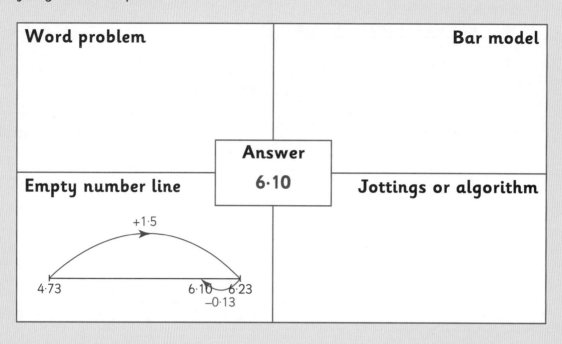

Word problem	Bar model
Answer 6·10	
Empty number line	**Jottings or algorithm**

+1·5
4·73   6·10   6·23
−0·13

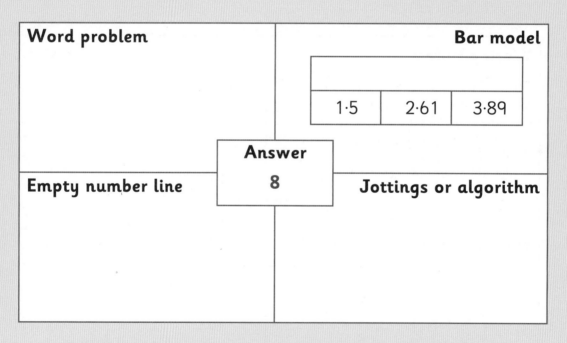

Word problem	Bar model
	1·5 2·61 3·89
Answer 8	
Empty number line	**Jottings or algorithm**

3.15 Multi-step word problems

1 In a school athletics competition, the winning time in the 100m relay was 53·93 seconds. Each team had four runners. In the winning team, the first three runners' times were 13·46 seconds, 13·20 seconds and 14·01 seconds. What was the fourth runner's time?

2 325m of fencing has been ordered for a children's petting zoo. 45·8m of fencing is needed for the small animal area. The picnic area and the play equipment area each need 84·6m of fencing. The car park needs 118·5m of fencing around it. Has enough fencing been ordered? Explain your answer.

3 The children are ordering pencils, pens and rulers to make up packs of equipment to sell at a school fair. Their order came to £203·28. The pencils cost £65·70 and the pens cost £11·95 more than the pencils. The rulers cost £17·72 less than the pens. How much was each item on the order?

4 Scientists at four Scottish weather stations measured the amount of rain that fell in July and got a combined total of 273·1mm. 71·55mm of rain was measured at Orkney and 49·28mm was measured at Dunbar. The scientists noticed that the amount of rain measured at Aviemore was double that of Dunbar. The fourth weather station was in Edinburgh. Work out how much rain was measured at the weather station in Edinburgh in July.

In this magic square, the numbers in each of the rows, columns and diagonals add up to 3·9. Fill in the blanks in the magic square.

0·66	0·6	0·24	1·38	
	0·72	0·36		1·44
	1·14	0·78		0·06
		1·2		0·48
	0·18		0·96	

1 Use the multiplication or division fact that is given to help you work out the answer to the problem. Two have been done for you.

a) $2 \times 7 = 14$, so $4 \times 7 =$ 28

b) $6 \times 7 = 42$, so $3 \times 7 =$ ___

c) $10 \times 7 = 70$, so $5 \times 7 =$ ___

d) $4 \times 7 = 28$, so $8 \times 7 =$ ___

e) $35 \div 7 = 5$, so $5 \times 7 =$ 35

f) $7 \times 7 = 49$, so ___ $\div 7 = 7$

g) $3 \times 7 = 21$, so ___ $\div 7 = 3$

h) $9 \times 7 = 63$, so ___ $\div 7 = 9$

2 Fill in the missing number in each of these.

a) $7 \times 4 =$ ___

b) $7 \times$ ___ $= 28$

c) $14 \div 7 =$ ___

d) $7 \times$ ___ $= 14$

e) $42 \div 7 =$ ___

f) ___ $\div 7 = 10$

g) $56 \div 7 =$ [ ]

h) [ ] $\times 7 = 14$

i) $12 \times 7 =$ [ ]

j) [ ] $\times 7 = 0$

k) [ ] $\div 7 = 6$

l) [ ] $\times 7 = 63$

3 We can use one 7s multiplication fact to work out other number facts, like this:

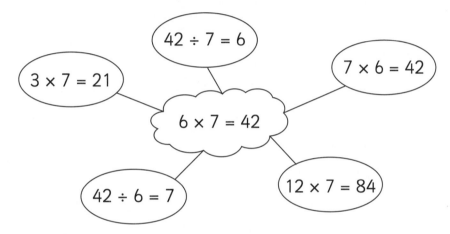

Add as many facts as you can in each of these.

a)

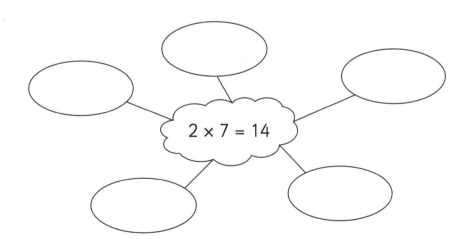

b)

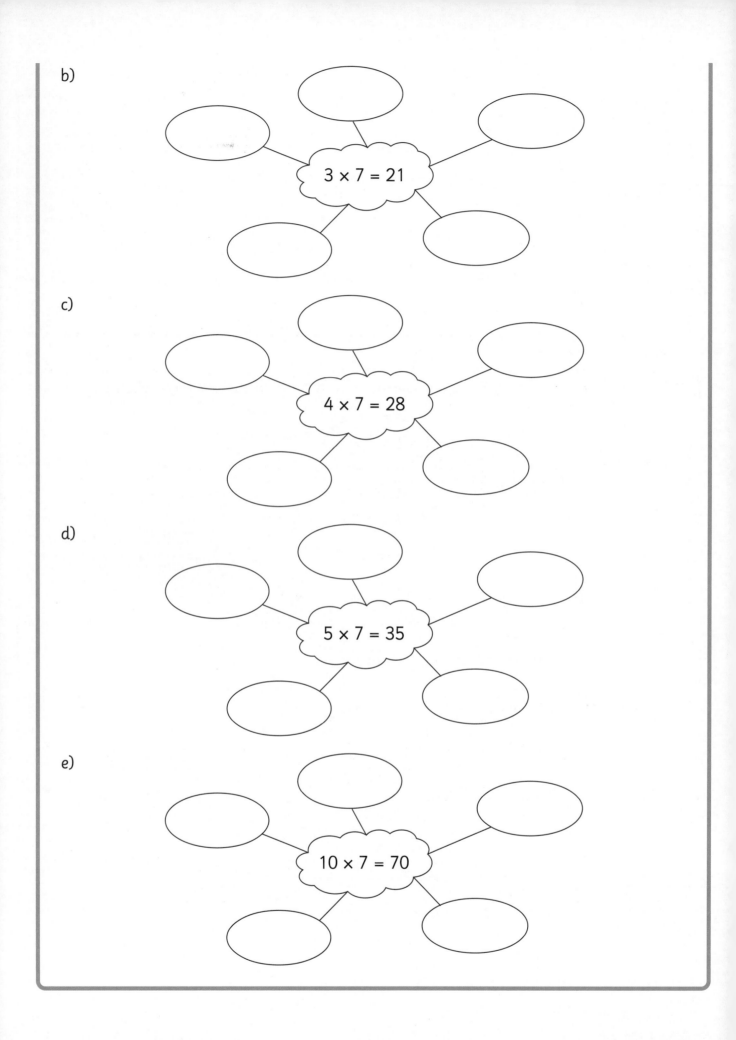

3 × 7 = 21

c)

4 × 7 = 28

d)

5 × 7 = 35

e)

10 × 7 = 70

1. Complete this number puzzle using 7s multiplication. You can only enter one digit or one symbol into each square.

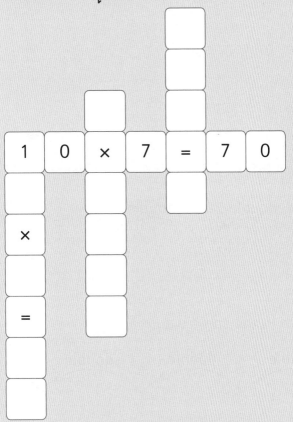

2. Can you find more than one way to complete the puzzle?

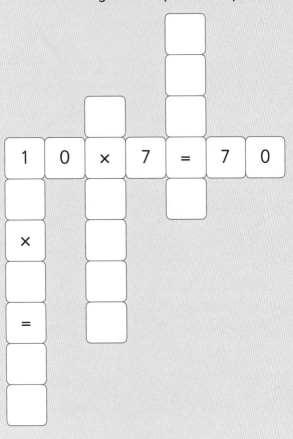

4.2 Recalling multiplication and division facts for 8

We can use the double-double-double method to help us when we are multiplying by 8. For example, to find 3 × 8 we begin by doubling 3:

3 × 2 = **6**

Then we double the answer to work out:

3 × 4 = **12**

We then double it again to work out:

3 × 8 = **24**

We can show the double-double-double strategy like this:

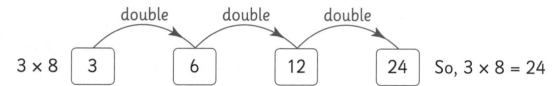

1. Complete each of these in the same way.

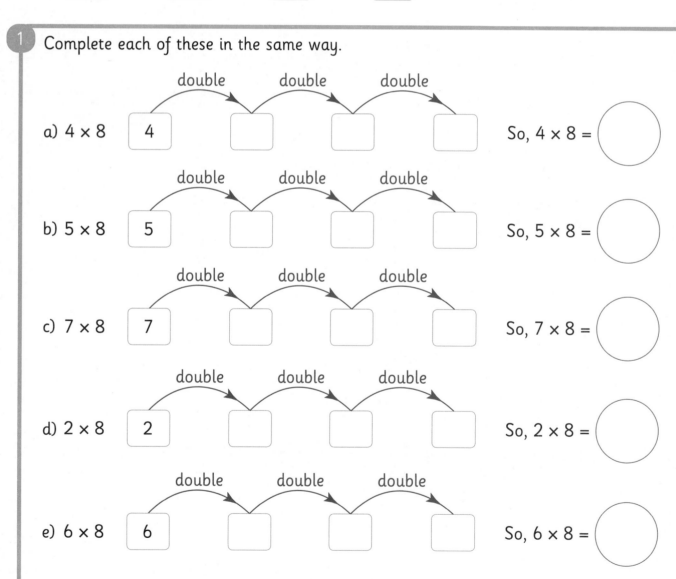

2 Complete these to work out the multiplication facts for 8. The first one has been done for you.

a) (5) × 8

double → double → double

| 5 | 10 | 20 | 40 | So, 5 × 8 = 40 |

b) ( ) × 8

double → double → double

| | | 12 | | So, |

c) ( ) × 8

double → double → double

| 8 | | | | So, |

d) ( ) × 8

double → double → double

| | 24 | | | So, |

e) ( ) × 8

double → double → double

| | | 28 | | So, |

f) ( ) × 8

double → double → double

| | | 44 | | So, |

3 We can write two multiplication facts and two division facts using the numbers in this triangle.

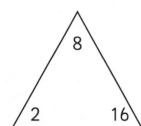

$2 \times 8 = 16$

$8 \times 2 = 16$

$16 \div 8 = 2$

$16 \div 2 = 8$

Use the numbers in these triangles to write two multiplication facts and two division facts.

a)

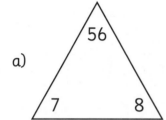

_____ × _____ = _____

_____ × _____ = _____

_____ ÷ _____ = _____

_____ ÷ _____ = _____

b)

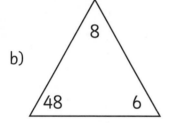

_____ × _____ = _____

_____ × _____ = _____

_____ ÷ _____ = _____

_____ ÷ _____ = _____

c)

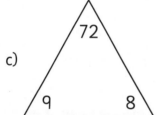

_____ × _____ = _____

_____ × _____ = _____

_____ ÷ _____ = _____

_____ ÷ _____ = _____

d)

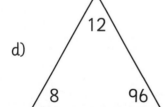

_____ × _____ = _____

_____ × _____ = _____

_____ ÷ _____ = _____

_____ ÷ _____ = _____

Work out how this multiplication wheel has been completed.

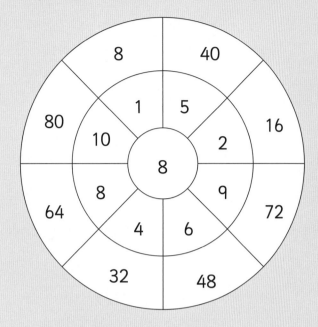

Now complete this multiplication wheel.

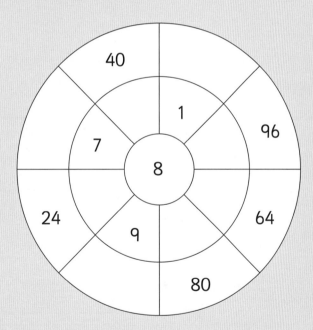

4.3 Multiplication with decimal fractions

1 Solve these problems:

a) 3·27 × 10 ⬚

b) 3·27 × 100 ⬚

c) 3·27 × 1000 ⬚

d) 0·04 × 10 ⬚

e) 0·04 × 100 ⬚

f) 0·04 × 1000 ⬚

g) 26·81 × 10 ⬚

h) 6·49 × 100 ⬚

i) 0·62 × 1000 ⬚

j) 84·67 × 100 ⬚

2 Circle True or False for each of these statements. Change one number in those that are false to make a true statement. Write this true statement in the space given.

a) 6·18 × 100 = 618   **True**   **False**

b) 0·47 × 10 = 47   **True**   **False**

c) 83·25 × 1000 = 8325   **True**   **False**

d) 0·13 × 10 = 1.3   **True**   **False**

e) 9·03 × 1000 = 9030   **True**   **False**

f) 194·3 × 100 = 1943   **True**   **False**

g) 1000 × 4·31 = 4000.31   **True**   **False**

h) 10 × 3266·45 = 326 645   **True**   **False**

3 What number should be under the splodge in each of these?

a) 1·96 × ![splodge] = 196

b) 14·72 × ![splodge] = 147·2

c) 49·94 × ![splodge] = 49 940

d) ![splodge] × 8·33 = 833

e) ![splodge] × 90·07 = 900·7

f) 0·199 × ![splodge] = 19·9

★ Challenge

Match each of these questions to its answer. One has been done for you.

Question	Answer
0·048 × 10	48
4·8 × 10	0·48
480 × 100	4·8
0·48 × 1000	4800
48 × 100	48 000
0·48 × 10	480

4.4 Division with decimal fractions

1 Solve these questions:

a) 83 ÷ 10

b) 83 ÷ 100

c) 83 ÷ 1000

d) 7 ÷ 10

e) 7 ÷ 100

f) 7 ÷ 1000

g) 30·71 ÷ 1000

h) 1·9 ÷ 100

2 Circle True or False for each of these statements. Change one number in those that are false to make a true statement. Write this true statement in the space given.

a) 304 ÷ 100 = 3·4   **True**   **False**

b) 0.58 ÷ 10 = 0·058   **True**   **False**

c) 15 467 ÷ 1000 = 1·5467   **True**   **False**

d) 25·53 ÷ 10 = 255·3   **True**   **False**

e) 195·4 ÷ 100 = 1·954   **True**   **False**

f) 1·88 ÷ 100 = 0·188   **True**   **False**

3 Fill in the missing numbers in each of these:

a) $45 \div \boxed{} = 0.45$

b) $\boxed{} \div 10 = 13.7$

c) $3400 \div \boxed{} = 3.4$

d) $1.54 \div \boxed{} = 0.154$

e) $\boxed{} \div 100 = 164.32$

f) $0.54 \div \boxed{} = 0.054$

★ Challenge

1. Fill in the missing numbers in these number machines.

$\boxed{} \xrightarrow{\div 1000} \boxed{} \xrightarrow{\times 2} \boxed{} \xrightarrow{\div 10} \boxed{\textbf{0.54}}$

$\boxed{} \xrightarrow{\div 10} \boxed{} \xrightarrow{\times 4} \boxed{} \xrightarrow{\div 100} \boxed{\textbf{1.68}}$

2. Now create two number machines of your own. The answers must be numbers that have tenths and hundredths in them.

$\boxed{} \xrightarrow{\div 1000} \boxed{} \xrightarrow{\times 2} \boxed{} \xrightarrow{\div 10} \boxed{}$

$\boxed{} \xrightarrow{\div 10} \boxed{} \xrightarrow{\times 4} \boxed{} \xrightarrow{\div 100} \boxed{}$

4.5 Solving multiplication problems

1 We can use the grid method to partition numbers by place value and solve multiplication problems. For example:

3216×4

×	3000	200	10	6
4	12000	800	40	24

$12000 + 800 + 40 + 24 = 12864$

Answer each of these questions using the grid method.

a) 5283×3

×				

b) 5283×8

×				

c) 1294×7

×				

d) 3294×7

×				

e) 6231 × 6

×				

f) 4883 × 5

×				

---

2 We can use brackets to partition numbers by place value and solve multiplication problems. For example:

$3216 × 4 = (3000 × 4) + (200 × 4) + (10 × 4) + (6 × 4)$

$= 12\,000 + 800 + 40 + 24$

$= 12\,864$

Answer these questions using brackets.

a) 4825 × 3

b) 4825 × 7

c) 6133 × 4

d) 2133 × 4

e) 8056 × 6

f) 2671 × 9

3

a) A bakery sells boxes of cupcakes. There are eight cupcakes in each box. If the bakery sells 2476 boxes in one day, how many cupcakes are sold altogether?

b) The bakery reduces the size of the cupcake boxes so that now there are only six cupcakes in each box. If the bakery sells 3281 boxes in a day, how many cupcakes are sold altogether?

c) A large order of cupcakes is packed into seven crates and loaded onto a van. If each crate contains 4913 boxes, how many boxes are there in the order altogether?

★ Challenge

This multiplication calculation uses each of these digits once.

| 0 | 1 | 2 | 3 | 4 | 5 | 6 | 7 | 8 | 9 |

Can you complete it?

| | | | 4 | × | 3 | = | | 7 | 0 | | |

4.6 Solving multiplication problems involving decimal fractions

1 We can use the grid method to partition decimal fractions by place value to make multiplying easier. For example:

6 × 8·23

×	8	0·2	0·03
6	48	1·2	0·18

48 + 1·2 + 0·18 = 49·38

Use the grid method to work out the answers to these problems.

a) 3 × 7·46

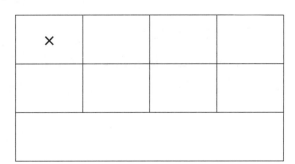

b) 8 × 7·46

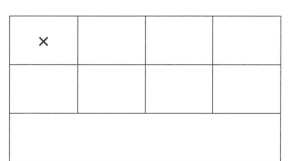

c) 8 × 4·32

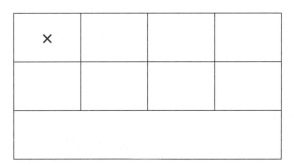

d) 5·44 × 6

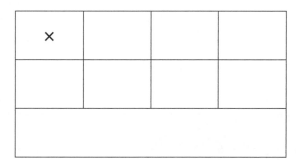

e) 1·87 × 4

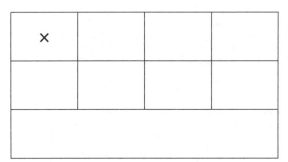

f) 3.7 × 9

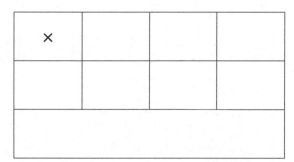

2 We can use brackets to partition decimal fractions by place value to make multiplying easier. For example:

$6 \times 8 \cdot 23 = (6 \times 8) + (6 \times 0 \cdot 2) + (6 \times 0 \cdot 03)$
$\qquad = 48 + 1 \cdot 2 + 0 \cdot 18$
$\qquad = 48 + 1 \cdot 38$
$\qquad = 49 \cdot 38$

Use brackets to work out the answers to these problems.

a) $6 \times 5 \cdot 83$

b) $6 \times 3 \cdot 83$

c) $4 \times 3 \cdot 83$

d) $6 \cdot 28 \times 7$

3 The children are ordering seeds to plant in the school garden. Work out the total cost for each of these collections.

Help us work out the cost.

a) Three packets of sunflower seeds at £2·34 per packet.

b) Eight packets of carrot seeds at £1·39 per packet.

c) Four packets of pumpkin seeds at £3·81 per packet.

d) Seven packets of radish seeds at £0·69 per packet.

e) Six packets of sweet pea seeds at £2·09 per packet.

★ Challenge

Can you find the multiplier in each of these input/output machines?
One has been done for you.

Input		Output
3·91	× 4	15·64
8·46		76·14
56·7		283·5
16·9		135·2
0·83		5·81

1 We can use the grid method to partition numbers by place value and solve division problems. For example:

415 ÷ 5

÷	400	10	5
5	80	2	1

80 + 2 + 1 = 83

Use the grid method to work out the answers to these problems.

a) 284 ÷ 4

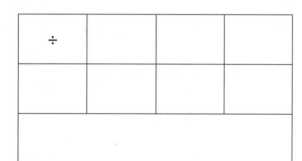

b) 468 ÷ 4

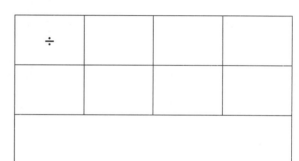

c) 366 ÷ 3

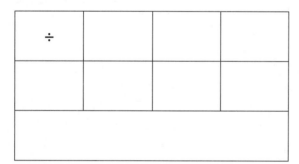

d) 633 ÷ 3

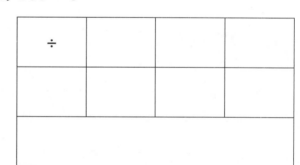

e) 945 ÷ 5

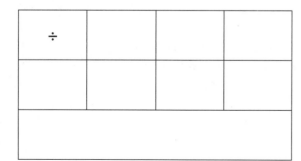

f) 396 ÷ 6

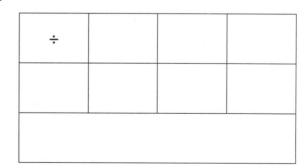

2 We can use multiplication facts that we know already to partition numbers and solve division problems. For example: $432 \div 6$

We know that 420 and 12 are both multiples of 6. We can then partition the 432 into 420 and 12 to make solving the problem easier.

$432 \div 6 = (420 \div 6) + (12 \div 6)$

$\qquad = 70 + 2$

$\qquad = 72$

Partition these numbers so that you can use multiplication facts. Then answer the calculation.

a) $365 \div 5$

b) $265 \div 5$

c) $256 \div 4$

d) $256 \div 8$

e) $642 \div 3$

f) $294 \div 7$

3 a) Choose your own strategy to divide these numbers by 9. Find the answers and say which strategy you used each time.

477	÷ 9 →		
288	÷ 9 →		
783	÷ 9 →		
612	÷ 9 →		

b) Choose your own strategy to divide these numbers by 8. Find the answer and say which strategy you used.

256	÷ 8 →		
472	÷ 8 →		
736	÷ 8 →		
504	÷ 8 →		

Challenge

The children are working together to find a number that can be divided exactly by 2, 3, 4, 5, 6, 7, 8 and 9.

I think 980 works.

No, it can't be 980.

1. Do you agree with Nuria? Explain why.

I think 2520 works.

2. Is Isla correct? Show your thinking for the number 2520.

We can double one factor and halve the other in a multiplication problem and the answer will not change. For example:

5 × 14

double | | halve

10 × 7   So 5 × 14 = 10 × 7 = 70

1 Find the answers to each of these using doubling and halving:

a) 3 × 18 [　　　]   b) 5 × 18 [　　　]

c) 4 × 22 [　　　]   d) 32 × 5 [　　　]

This also works for tripling and thirding. For example:

4 × 27

triple | | third

12 × 9   So 4 × 27 = 12 × 9 = 108

2 Find the answers to each of these using tripling and thirding:

a) 3 × 18 [　　　]   b) 5 × 12 [　　　]

c) 6 × 15 [　　　]   d) 27 × 3 [　　　]

3 Use doubling and halving, or tripling and thirding, to help you solve these problems. Explain how you worked out each problem.

a) 16 sports tops were bought for school teams to use. Each top cost £7 How much did the tops cost altogether?

b) 21 tickets for a special screening at the cinema were bought for a youth club. Each ticket cost £4. How much did the tickets cost altogether?

c) Lunch boxes were packed into crates to take on a school outing. Each crate had 26 lunch boxes in it and there were five crates in total. How many lunch boxes were there altogether?

★ Challenge

How many pairs of equal calculations can you find here? Join these up by drawing a line between them. One has been done for you.

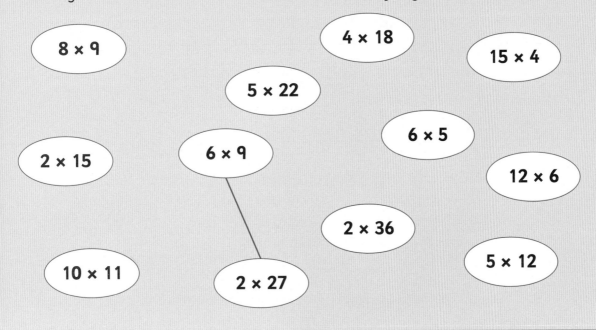

8 × 9

4 × 18

15 × 4

5 × 22

6 × 5

2 × 15

6 × 9

12 × 6

2 × 36

10 × 11

2 × 27

5 × 12

4.9 Solving division problems

1 Solve the following problems by rounding and compensating. The first one has been done for you.

a) $56 \div 4 =$ | $(60 \div 4) - (4 \div 4)$ | $=$ | $15 - 1 = 14$

b) $81 \div 3 =$ | | $=$ |

c) $92 \div 4 =$ | | $=$ |

d) $57 \div 3 =$ | | $=$ |

e) $145 \div 5 =$ | | $=$ |

2 Eggs are being packed into boxes. Each box will have six eggs in it. Use rounding and compensating to work out how many boxes will be needed for 84 eggs.

3

a) Amman, Finlay, Isla and Nuria are working together on an art project. Their teacher gives them 68 lollipop sticks to use in the project and they decide to share them equally. Use rounding and compensating to work out how many lollipop sticks each of the children will get.

b) Another pupil joins the children so the group now has five children in it. The teacher gives them an extra 27 lollipop sticks so they now have 95 altogether. Use rounding and compensating to work out how many lollipop sticks each child will get if they share them equally.

Finlay thinks that the answer to each of these division problems is the same, but Amman disagrees. He says, "One of them is different."
Do you agree with Finlay or Amman? Explain your answer.

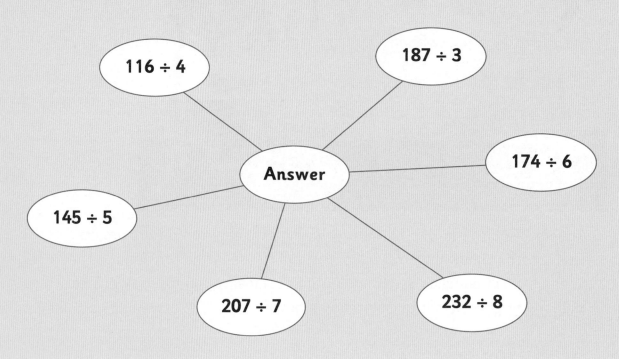

1 We can use the grid method to partition numbers to make multiplying easier. Complete these multiplication questions to find the answer.

a) 13 × 36

×	10	3
30		
6		

b) 23 × 36

×		

c) 23 × 46

×		

d) 23 × 44

×		

e) 64 × 28

×		

f) 53 × 37

×		

2 We can use a standard algorithm for multiplication to help us solve multiplication problems that are too challenging to solve mentally. For example:

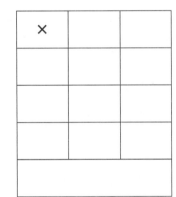

23 × 36

(36 × 3)
(36 × 20)

$$\begin{array}{r} 36 \\ \times\ 23 \\ \hline 108 \\ 720 \\ \hline 828 \end{array}$$

Use the standard written method to solve these problems.

a) 32 × 43

b) 22 × 46

c) 41 × 29

3 Choose either the grid method or the standard written algorithm to solve each of these problems.

a) 14 boxes each contain 24 pencils. How many pencils are there altogether?

b) A theatre has 32 rows of seats with 26 seats in each row. How many seats are there altogether in the theatre?

Use the clues to complete this cross-number puzzle. Each box in the completed puzzle will only have one digit in it.

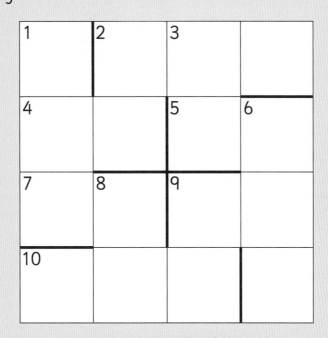

Across

2) 32 × 30 =

4) 11 × [   ] = 121

5) 10 × [   ] = 710

7) 13 × 7 =

9) [   ] × 12 = 780

10) 79 × 4 =

Down

1) 21 × 39 =

2) 7 × 13 =

3) 11 × [   ] = 737

6) [   ] × 2 = 316

8) 5 × [   ] = 55

9) 13 × [   ] = 858

1 Use the written method to solve these division problems:

a) 4) 9 2   b) 4) 7 2   c) 3) 7 2

2 Work out the answer to these problems using the written form:

a) 95 ÷ 5

b) 135 ÷ 5

c) 185 ÷ 5

d) 168 ÷ 3

e) 152 ÷ 4

f) 203 ÷ 7

3 A craft group knitted 224 baby hats to donate to a local hospital. The hats are going to be packed into boxes before they are taken to the hospital. Use the written method to work out how many boxes will be needed if each box contains:

a) 4 hats

b) 7 hats

c) 8 hats

The children are playing a game. They are trying to throw plastic balls into a large bowl. Each time they get a ball into the bowl they score 9 points. This table shows how many points each child scored.

Amman	234
Finlay	153
Isla	207
Nuria	261

Can you work out how many balls each child got into the bowl?

1 Use the written method to work out the answers to these problems.

a) $4\overline{)7 \cdot 2\,6}$ b) $3\overline{)5 \cdot 2\,8}$ c) $4\overline{)6 \cdot 1\,2}$

2 Work out the answer to these problems using the written form:

a) 1·38 ÷ 3

b) 2·67 ÷ 3

c) 3·48 ÷ 6

d) 4·62 ÷ 6

e) 1·33 ÷ 7

f) 4·96 ÷ 8

3 The children and their teacher are going to make soup. They go shopping for vegetables and this is their receipt.

CASH RECEIPT
Any Day Supermarket

Address:	5 High Street
Tel:	124 905 7385
Manager:	Noah Kane

4 large turnips	£4.92
9 carrots	£1.17
6 large potatoes	£7.38
2 leeks	£1.14
4 onions	£1.52
7 parsnips	£4.83

Price	£20.96
Sale	£3.96
Tax	£5.12

Total	£30.24

Thank you for shopping!!!

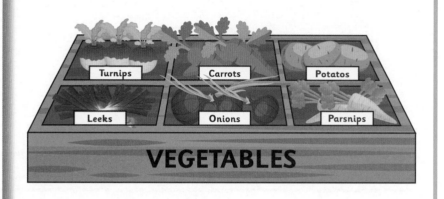

VEGETABLES

Work out the cost of:

a) one large turnip

b) one carrot

c) one large potato

d) one leek

e) one onion

f) one parsnip

★ Challenge

Work out the missing digits in these calculations.

$$1 \cdot 5\,\boxed{}$$
$$4\,)\,\boxed{} \cdot 1\ 2$$

$$1 \cdot 7\,\boxed{}$$
$$2\,)\,\boxed{} \cdot 2\ \boxed{5}$$

1 Find the answer to these problems using the order of operations. Use brackets to show how you solved each problem. Two of the problems have been solved for you.

a) 6 × 4 + 5

= (6 × 4) + 5

= 24 + 5

= 29

b) 6 + 4 × 5

c) 6 + 4 × 5 − 3

d) 6 ÷ 3 + 12

= (6 ÷ 3) + 12

= 2 + 12

= 14

e) 8 + 6 ÷ 3 − 1

f) 35 ÷ 7 + 20 − 6

g) 18 − 5 × 3 + 26

h) 29 + 4 × 6 − 15 ÷ 5

i) 28 ÷ 4 + 3 × 9 − 5

2 The answer given for each of these problems is incorrect. Use brackets and the order of operations to help you to find the errors, then work out the correct answer to each problem.

a) $18 + 9 \div 3 = 27 \div 3 = 9$

b) $4 \times 5 + 2 \times 3 = 22 \times 3 = 66$

c) $37 - 7 \times 3 + 8 = 37 - 21 + 8 = 8$

d) $60 - 15 \div 3 + 2 \times 4 = 45 \div 3 + 8 = 22$

3 Write +, −, x or ÷ in each blank box so that each number sentence balances.

a) 4 ☐ 4 ☐ 3 = 16

b) 4 ☐ 6 ☐ 4 = 20

c) 4 ☐ 3 ☐ 3 = 13

d) 5 ☐ 4 ☐ 4 = 21

★ Challenge

1. Using each of the digits 4, 6, 7 and 8 once in this problem, what is the greatest answer you can find?

 + × − ☐ =

2. Using each of the digits 4, 6, 7 and 8 once in this problem, what is the smallest answer you can find?

☐ + ☐ × ☐ − ☐ = ☐

5.1 Using knowledge of multiples and factors to work out divisibility rules

We know these divisibility rules:

A number will be divisible by

2	IF	the last digit is an even number, including zero
3	IF	the sum of the digits is a multiple of three
4	IF	the sum of the last two digits can be divided by four
5	IF	the last digit is zero or five
6	IF	the number is divisible by two **and** by three
8	IF	the sum of the last three digits is divisible by eight
9	IF	the sum of the digits is a multiple of nine
10	IF	the last digit is a zero

1 Write each of these numbers into the correct column in the table. Two have been done for you.

2312   3565   4158   4768   6246

6744   7808   8563   10 128   14 566

Divisible by 8	Not divisible by 8
2312	3565

2

a) Are these numbers divisible by 6? Circle all the numbers that can be divided exactly by 6.

254	336	521	582	690	879

1482	2581	3564	5892	21246	28136

3

Use the divisibility rules to work out if these statements are true or false. Circle **True** or **False** for each one and say why you have circled this. The first one has been done for you.

a) 684 is divisible by 3   (**True**)   **False**

6 + 8 + 4 = 18. This is a multiple of 3 so 684 is divisible by 3.

b) 684 is divisible by 9   **True**   **False**

c) 4575 is divisible by 4   **True**   **False**

d) 4575 is divisible by 5   **True**   **False**

e) 12670 is divisible by 10   **True**   **False**

f) 12670 is divisible by 8 **True** **False**

g) 3414 is divisible by 6 **True** **False**

h) 8577 is divisible by 9 **True** **False**

★ Challenge

1. Use these clues to find the mystery number:
   - ❖ It is a three-digit number
   - ❖ It is divisible by 7
   - ❖ It is not divisible by 2
   - ❖ The sum of its digits is 4

2. Use these clues to find the mystery number:
   - ❖ It is a three-digit number less than 300
   - ❖ It is divisible by 2 and 5
   - ❖ It is not divisible by 3
   - ❖ The sum of its digits is 7

1 A tennis club has 285 tennis balls that need to be put into tins for storage.

a) Each tin holds four tennis balls. Will the tennis balls all fit into the tins with none left over? How do you know?

b) How many tins will be needed altogether for the tennis balls?

c) If instead the club buy tins that hold 6 tennis balls, how many tins would be needed for the tennis balls?

2 The answers given for each of these calculations is incorrect. Use your knowledge of factors and multiples to explain why the answers cannot be correct. The first one has been done for you.

Calculation	Reason why the answer is incorrect
68 × 5 = 304	Multiples of 5 always end in 0 or a 5, not 4.
46 × 3 = 448	
280 × 9 = 2510	
265 ÷ 2 = 130·5	
424 ÷ 6 = 69	

3 A gardener has 48 paving slabs and is going to lay them in a rectangle in a new garden. The rectangle can be any length and width. Use your knowledge of factors to work out all the possible ways the gardener can lay all 48 paving slabs in the garden.

⭐ **Challenge**

Find the missing factors to complete these multiplication squares.

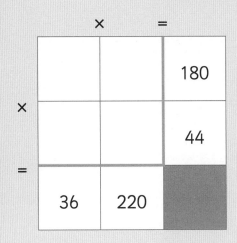

	×		=
×			60
	12		36
=	48	45	

	×		=
×			180
			44
=	36	220